A Wise Ape Teaches Kindness

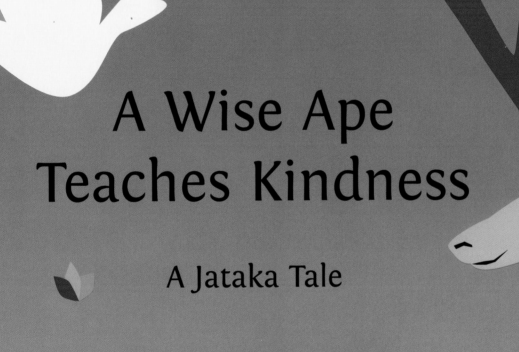

A Wise Ape
Teaches Kindness

A Jataka Tale

Illustrated by Andrea Kassof

Dharma Publishing

Jataka Tales Series

Second edition 2009, revised and augmented with guidance for parents and teachers.
Cover design by Kando Dorsey.

Printed on acid-free paper.

Printed in the United States of America by Dharma Press
35788 Hauser Bridge Road, Cazadero, California 95421.

9   8   7   6   5   4   3   2

Library of Congress Control Number: 2009938987
ISBN 978-0-89800-519-6

www.dharmapublishing.com

Dedicated to children everywhere

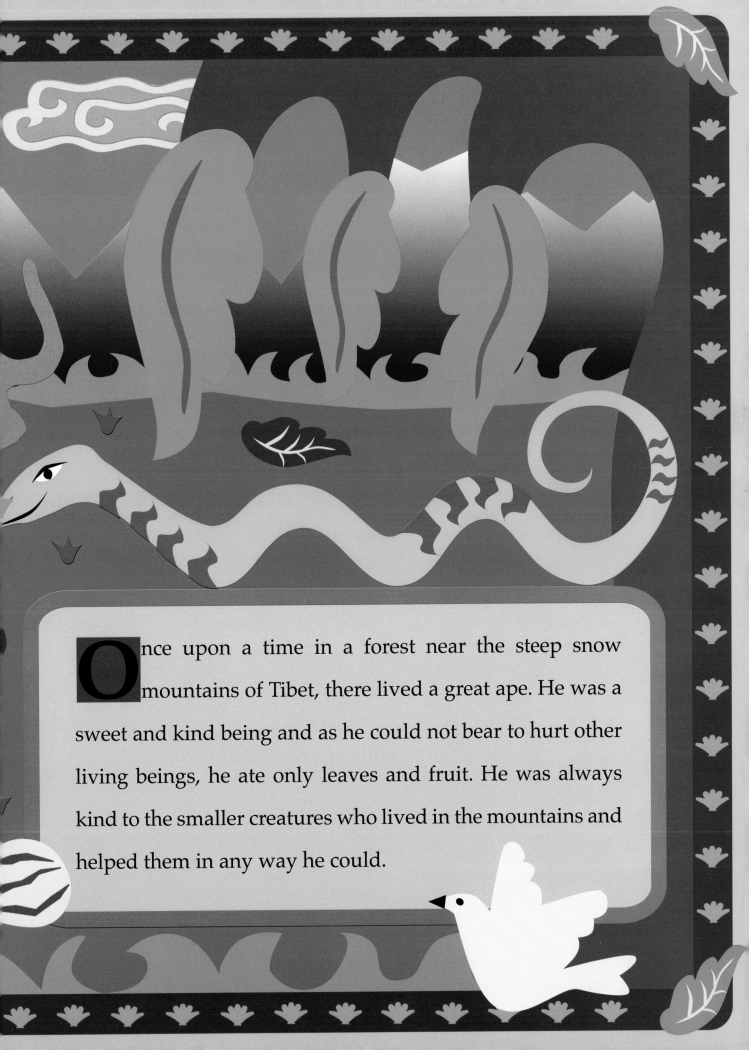

Once upon a time in a forest near the steep snow mountains of Tibet, there lived a great ape. He was a sweet and kind being and as he could not bear to hurt other living beings, he ate only leaves and fruit. He was always kind to the smaller creatures who lived in the mountains and helped them in any way he could.

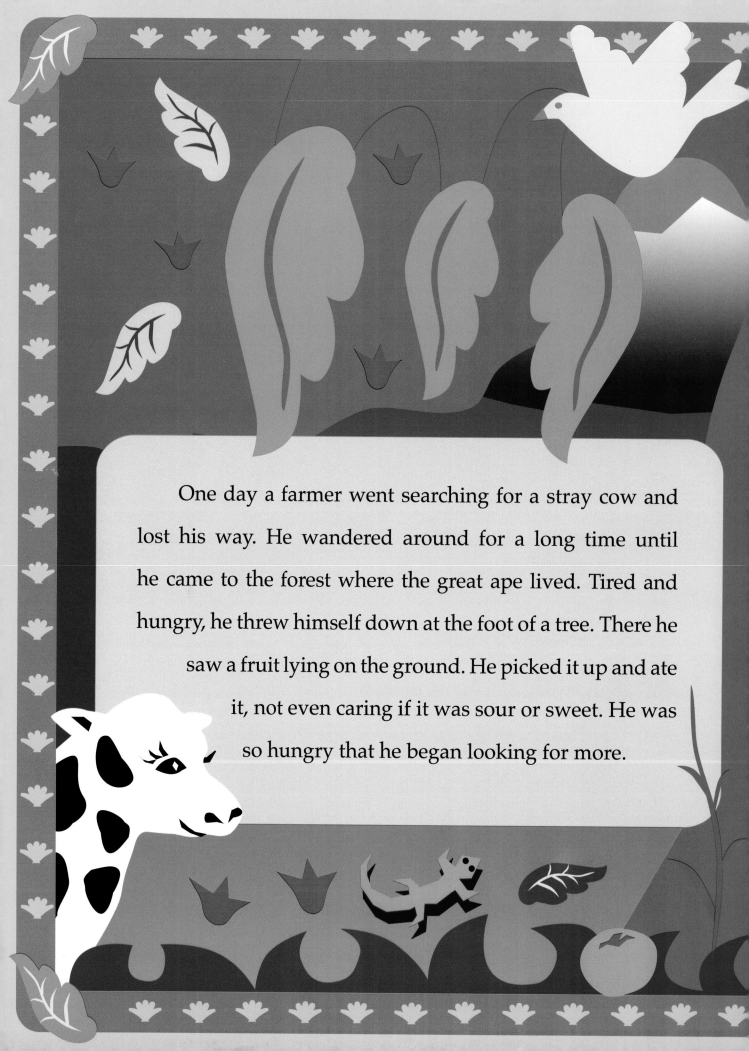

One day a farmer went searching for a stray cow and lost his way. He wandered around for a long time until he came to the forest where the great ape lived. Tired and hungry, he threw himself down at the foot of a tree. There he saw a fruit lying on the ground. He picked it up and ate it, not even caring if it was sour or sweet. He was so hungry that he began looking for more.

Looking up, he saw the fruit tree growing out of a rocky slope at the edge of a waterfall; its branches loaded with fruit hung out over the cliff. The farmer scrambled up the slope and then climbed the tree until he reached a branch heavy with fruit. He was so eager to get to the golden fruit that he crawled out to the very end of the branch.

Suddenly the branch broke, and with a cry the farmer tumbled headlong over the cliff, holding onto the branch for dear life. He fell down a long way into a pool of water at the bottom of the ravine. The leaves of the branch had cushioned his fall, and he was unharmed. When he climbed out of the cold water, he looked around. There were steep rock walls all around the dark pit, and he could not see any way to get out.

Days went by while the farmer was alone in the dark pit. He drank water from the pool and ate the few pieces of fruit that had fallen in the water with him. One day the great ape happened to pass through that part of the forest in search of food. He too climbed the large fruit tree. When he looked down over the waterfall, far below him he saw the man lying at the bottom of the ravine. Forgetting his own search for food, he called out, "You there, what are you doing down there? Who are you and what has happened to you?"

"I am a poor farmer and I lost my way in the forest," the farmer cried, weak with hunger. "I tried to pick fruit from that tree and fell down into this terrible place. I am all alone and have no friends who will come find me. Please rescue me or I will die here!"

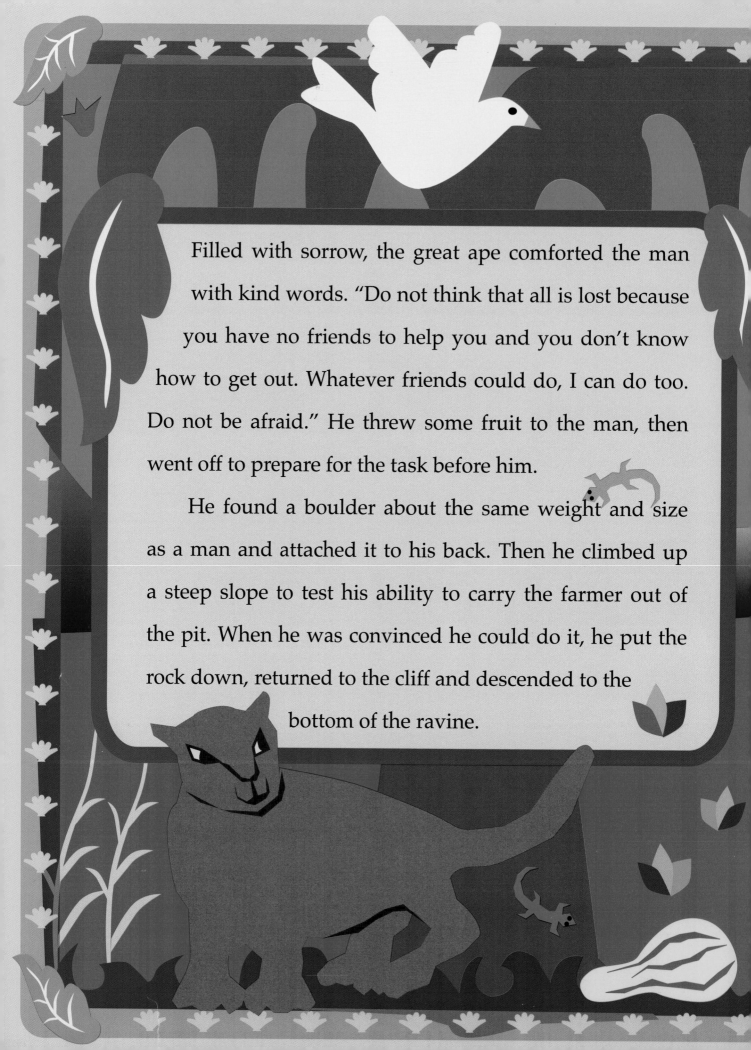

Filled with sorrow, the great ape comforted the man with kind words. "Do not think that all is lost because you have no friends to help you and you don't know how to get out. Whatever friends could do, I can do too. Do not be afraid." He threw some fruit to the man, then went off to prepare for the task before him.

He found a boulder about the same weight and size as a man and attached it to his back. Then he climbed up a steep slope to test his ability to carry the farmer out of the pit. When he was convinced he could do it, he put the rock down, returned to the cliff and descended to the bottom of the ravine.

He said gently to the farmer, "Climb up on my back and hold on tightly to me."

Relieved, the farmer mounted on the great ape's back and put his arms around his neck. The great ape, stooping with the weight of his burden, climbed with great difficulty up the steep walls of the pit.

At the top of the cliff, the farmer slid off the ape's back. The great ape was so exhausted that he lay down to rest. He said to the farmer, "This part of the forest is full of wild animals. While I sleep, please keep watch over us both."

"Do not fear," the man promised. "I will stay here and guard both of us. Sleep as long as you like."

As soon as the great ape had fallen asleep, evil thoughts sprang up in the farmer's mind. "Why should I stay here?" he thought. "There is nothing to eat in this place but roots and fruit. How can I ever escape from this forest if I don't recover my strength? The body of this ape would give me more than enough food for my journey. There is no time to lose – I must kill him while he is asleep. Once he wakes up, not even a lion could kill him."

The man's mind was so caught up in dark thoughts that he completely forgot his feelings of gratitude. He took up a large stone and aimed at the great ape's head.

But the farmer was weak from hunger and hardship, and when he threw the stone, it only bruised the great ape's temple, then fell to the ground with a loud thud.

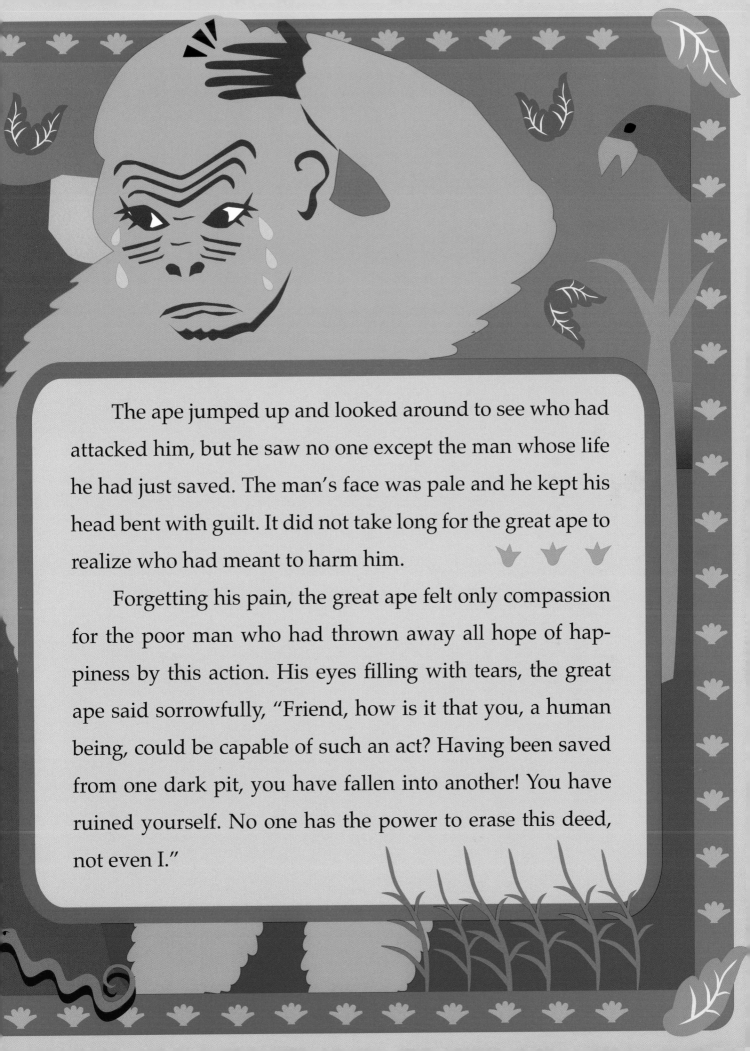

The ape jumped up and looked around to see who had attacked him, but he saw no one except the man whose life he had just saved. The man's face was pale and he kept his head bent with guilt. It did not take long for the great ape to realize who had meant to harm him.

Forgetting his pain, the great ape felt only compassion for the poor man who had thrown away all hope of happiness by this action. His eyes filling with tears, the great ape said sorrowfully, "Friend, how is it that you, a human being, could be capable of such an act? Having been saved from one dark pit, you have fallen into another! You have ruined yourself. No one has the power to erase this deed, not even I."

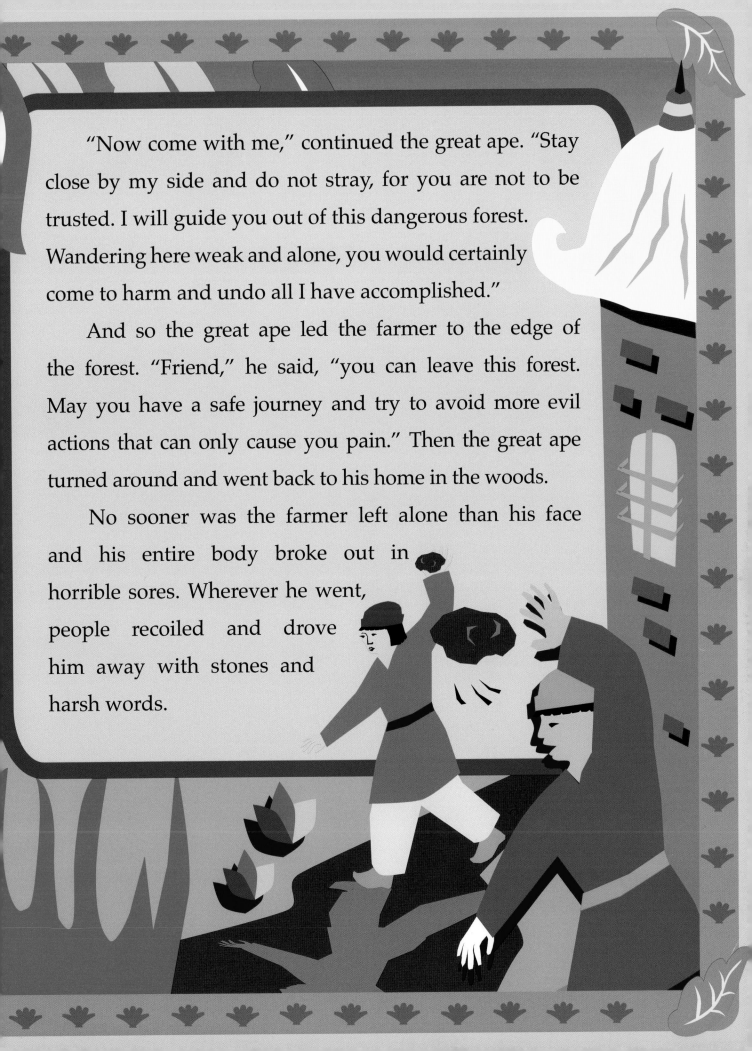

"Now come with me," continued the great ape. "Stay close by my side and do not stray, for you are not to be trusted. I will guide you out of this dangerous forest. Wandering here weak and alone, you would certainly come to harm and undo all I have accomplished."

And so the great ape led the farmer to the edge of the forest. "Friend," he said, "you can leave this forest. May you have a safe journey and try to avoid more evil actions that can only cause you pain." Then the great ape turned around and went back to his home in the woods.

No sooner was the farmer left alone than his face and his entire body broke out in horrible sores. Wherever he went, people recoiled and drove him away with stones and harsh words.

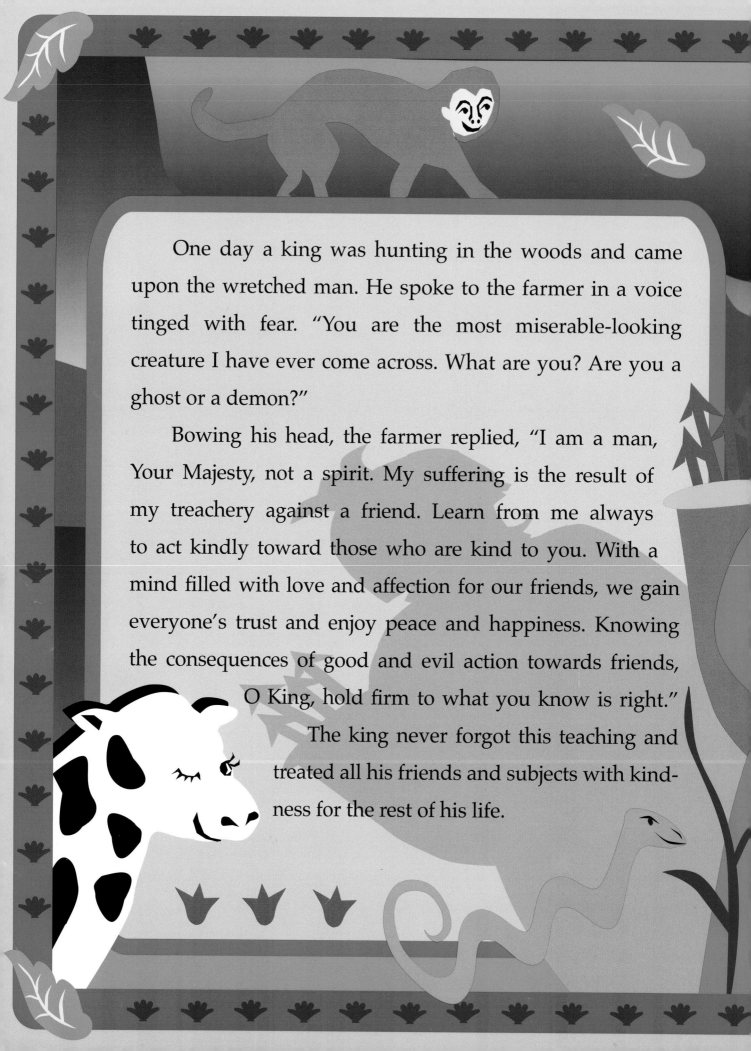

One day a king was hunting in the woods and came upon the wretched man. He spoke to the farmer in a voice tinged with fear. "You are the most miserable-looking creature I have ever come across. What are you? Are you a ghost or a demon?"

Bowing his head, the farmer replied, "I am a man, Your Majesty, not a spirit. My suffering is the result of my treachery against a friend. Learn from me always to act kindly toward those who are kind to you. With a mind filled with love and affection for our friends, we gain everyone's trust and enjoy peace and happiness. Knowing the consequences of good and evil action towards friends, O King, hold firm to what you know is right."

The king never forgot this teaching and treated all his friends and subjects with kindness for the rest of his life.

The Jataka Tales nurture in readers young and old an appreciation for values shared by all the world's great traditions. Read aloud, performed and studied for centuries, they communicate universal values such as kindness, forgiveness, compassion, humility, courage, honesty and patience. You can bring these stories alive through the suggestions on these pages. Actively engaging with the stories creates a bridge to the children in your life and opens a dialogue about what brings joy, stability and caring.

A Wise Ape Teaches Kindness

A hungry farmer searching for his missing cow loses his way in the forest and falls into a deep ravine. The man is rescued by an ape. When the ape is tired and wants to rest, he asks the man to guard him. The ungrateful farmer tries to kill his sleeping rescuer. Still, the ape feels compassion for the farmer and brings him to safety. Later, having learned the consequences of good and evil actions toward friends, the farmer teaches a king to treat everyone with kindness.

Key Values
Kindness
Knowing the power of thoughts and actions
Helping others

Bringing the story to life

Engage the children by saying, "This story takes place in a deep forest where a great ape lives. One day a farmer gets lost and falls into a pit. What do you think happens to him? Let's read to find out."

- How did the farmer end up in the pit?
- What does the ape do when he finds the farmer?
- How does the farmer treat the ape after he has been rescued? Why?
- How does the ape respond to the ungrateful farmer? How do you feel about that?
- What happens to the man after he returns home?
- Why does the king question the farmer? Why is the king changed?

Discussion topics and questions can be modified depending on the child's age.

Teaching values through play

Follow up on the storytelling with creative activities that explore the characters and values and appeal to the five senses.

- Have children construct and decorate character masks for the ape, the farmer and the king. Act out the story, and have them switch roles. Ask the children if they would help a friend who tried to hurt them after they protected him. What if they were a king? Ask why the great ape saves the farmer twice.

- The children can play at being skilled, useful adults who help others and learn how to be loyal friends. Remind them that the ape trains to save the farmer by carrying a rock on his back, and that the ape remains a friend to the farmer even when the farmer treats him badly. Let them play a fireperson, a coach, a doctor, teacher, a president, a bus driver.

- Have the children make a ravine out of blankets or a dark corner of a room. They can go to this place to explore what it is like being trapped in a dark place. One child can remain outside and can pull the other one out with a kind word, a happy song, or a positive action (or the power of a king!). Children can trade roles.

- Children can make up various endings, such as one where the farmer struggles with his fears, overcomes his dark thoughts and watches over the sleeping ape.

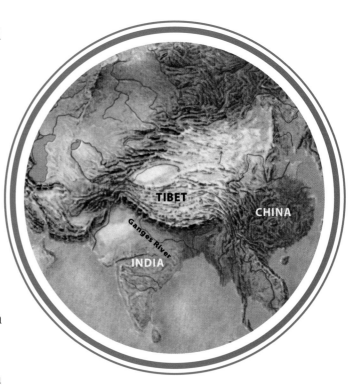

Active reading

- Before children can read, they love growing familiar with characters and drawings. You can show them the pictures and tell the story in your own words with characteristic voices for the ape, farmer and king.

- Carry a book whenever you leave the house in case there is some extra time for reading.

Daily activities

- Display the key values on the refrigerator or a bulletin board – at child's eye level – and refer to them in your daily interactions.

- Ask what makes a good friend. Can friends forgive each other?

- Children can practice becoming a good friend by listening to someone without interrupting and, in turn, feel what it is like to be listened to.

- When you visit the zoo, notice how the apes groom each other and how the mothers take care of the little ones.

- Ask the children about a time when someone treated them with kindness even when they were angry or upset. See if the children can remember when they began to appreciate that caring treatment.

We are grateful for the opportunity to offer these Jataka Tales to you. May they inspire fresh insight into the dynamics of human relationships and may understanding grow with each reading.

This adaptation of a Jataka Tale is for children aged five to nine

JATAKA TALES SERIES